NORTHBROOK PUBLIC LIBRARY
1201 CEDAR LANE
NORTHBROOK, ILL 60062

Northbrook Public Library

DISCARDED

3 1123 00924 4248

W9-AAX-551

# Cougars

### By JoAnn Early Macken

**Reading Consultant:** Jeanne Clidas, Ph.D.
Director, Roberts Wesleyan College Literacy Clinic

**WEEKLY READER®**

PUBLISHING

Please visit our web site at **www.garethstevens.com**.
For a free catalog describing our list of high-quality books,
call 1-877-542-2595 (USA) or 1-800-387-3178 (Canada).
Our fax: 1-877-542-2596

**Library of Congress Cataloging-in-Publication Data**

Macken, JoAnn Early, 1953–
        Cougars / by JoAnn Early Macken. — [Rev. ed.]
            p. cm. — (Animals that live in the mountains)
        Includes bibliographical references and index.
        ISBN-10: 1-4339-2411-0    ISBN-13: 978-1-4339-2411-8 (lib. bdg.)
        ISBN-10: 1-4339-2494-3    ISBN-13: 978-1-4339-2494-1 (soft cover)
        1. Puma—Juvenile literature. I. Title.
    QL737.C23M174    2009
    599.75'24—dc22                                    2009000102

This edition first published in 2010 by
**Weekly Reader® Books**
An Imprint of Gareth Stevens Publishing
1 Reader's Digest Road
Pleasantville, NY  10570-7000 USA

Copyright © 2010 by Gareth Stevens, Inc.

Executive Managing Editor: Lisa M. Herrington
Senior Editor: Barbara Bakowski
Project Management: Spooky Cheetah Press
Cover Designers: Jennifer Ryder-Talbot and Studio Montage
Production: Studio Montage
Library Consultant: Carl Harvey, Library Media Specialist, Noblesville, Indiana

Photo credits: Cover, pp. 1, 9 Shutterstock; pp. 5, 7, 15, 21 © Tom and Pat Leeson; pp. 11, 19 © Michael H. Francis;
p. 13 © Alan and Sandy Carey; p. 17 © Richard Day/Daybreak Imagery

All rights reserved. No part of this book may be reproduced, stored in a retrieval system,
or transmitted in any form or by any means, electronic, mechanical, photocopying, recording,
or otherwise, without the prior written permission of the copyright holder. For permission, contact
**permissions@gspub.com**.

Printed in the United States of America

1 2 3 4 5 6 7 8 9 14 13 12 11 10 09

# Table of Contents

**Boldface** words appear in the glossary.

## Baby Cougars

A baby cougar is a **cub**. Cougar cubs have spots on their fur.

cub

Cougars are **mammals**. Mammals drink milk from their mothers. The cubs start to eat meat in about a month.

Like kittens, cubs like to play.
They are good climbers. At
two months old, they learn
how to hunt. They are on
their own at two years old.

## Built for Success

A grown cougar is mostly tan or gray. A cougar's fur blends in with trees and the ground.

cougar

Cougars can leap high and far. Their long tails help them balance.

## On the Hunt

Cougars hunt alone. They hide behind rocks and trees. They creep up on their **prey** and pounce.

prey

Cougars hunt deer and other animals. They often leap onto their prey from above. They hunt from cliffs or high ledges.

After they eat, cougars cover their prey with leaves, dirt, or snow. They come back later to eat more.

Cougars do not roar like other big cats. They **snarl**, hiss, and purr. Cougars are known by many other names. They are also called pumas, panthers, or mountain lions.

# Fast Facts

| | |
|---|---|
| **Height** | about 2 feet (61 centimeters) at the shoulder |
| **Length** | about 9 feet (3 meters) nose to tail |
| **Weight** | Males: about 200 pounds (91 kilograms)<br>Females: about 130 pounds (59 kilograms) |
| **Diet** | mainly deer, but also smaller animals |
| **Average life span** | up to 12 years |

# Glossary

**cub:** a baby cougar or other animal

**mammals:** animals that give birth to live babies and feed them milk

**prey:** animals that are killed for food

**snarl:** to growl and bare the teeth

# For More Information

## Books

*Cougars.* In the Wild (series). Stephanie St. Pierre (Heinemann, 2001)

*Cougars.* Wildcats! of North America (series). Jalma Barrett (Blackbirch Press, 2007)

## Web Sites

### Cougar
*www.nps.gov/ccso/cougar.htm*
Learn more about these big cats.

### Cougars
www.*wdfw.wa.gov/wlm/living/cougars.htm*
View closeup photos of cougar paws, claws, and tracks.

**Publisher's note to educators and parents:** Our editors have carefully reviewed these web sites to ensure that they are suitable for children. Many web sites change frequently, however, and we cannot guarantee that a site's future contents will continue to meet our high standards of quality and educational value. Be advised that children should be closely supervised whenever they access the Internet.

# Index

# About the Author

JoAnn Early Macken is the author of two rhyming picture books, *Sing-Along Song* and *Cats on Judy*, and more than 80 nonfiction books for children. Her poems have appeared in several children's magazines. She lives in Wisconsin with her husband and their two sons.